the
SOCIAL SKILLS
handbook

PRACTICAL ACTIVITIES FOR SOCIAL COMMUNICATION

SUE HUTCHINGS • JAYNE COMINS • JUDY OFFILER

D0154640

Speechmark Publishing Ltd
Telford Road, Bicester, Oxon OX26 4LQ, UK

Published by

Speechmark Publishing Ltd, Telford Road, Bicester, Oxon OX26 4LQ,
United Kingdom
Telephone: +44 (0) 1869 244 644   Facsimile: +44 (0) 1869 320 040
www.speechmark.net

002-0670/Printed in Great Britain/1010

British Library Cataloguing in Publication Data
Hutchings, Sue
    The social skills handbook: practical activities for social communication
    1. Social skills – children   2. Education – special education   3. Social
    communication
    I. Title   II. Comins, Jayne   III. Offiler, Judy
    302.07

ISBN 0 86388 368 0
(Previously published by Winslow Press Ltd under ISBN 0 86388 089 4)

CONTENTS

SUE HUTCHINGS is currently working as a lecturer at Dorset House School of Occupational Therapy, Oxford. A professional interest in social communication skills has mainly developed from an educational perspective. Previously, she has worked as an occupational therapist in mental health, both in a psychiatric hospital and in the community.

JAYNE COMINS has skills in speech therapy, counselling and occupational and organizational psychology. She is currently Information Officer at the College of Speech and Language Therapists and specializes in voice disorders at The Royal National Throat, Nose and Ear Hospital, London. She has experience of organizing and running groups in hospitals, homes and day centres and helped to establish a mental health team assisting clients back into the community.

JUDY OFFILER is an experienced speech therapist who developed an interest in social communication skills particularly through her last post in London, which involved working in 'Care in the Community' projects with adults who have a learning difficulty. She is now employed by South Tees Health Authority and continues to work with clients who have learning difficulties.

FOREWORD

Social skills training (SST) is becoming increasingly popular, and there is a great need for it. Many mentally-ill patients have problems which are mainly in the area of social behaviour or relationships, for example 25–30% of adult neurotics. In the general population there are many people who cannot make friends, or who cannot cope with the opposite sex, or who say that they are 'shy' or 'lonely'. These people are isolated and unhappy through lack of social skills.

Social skills are important at work. SST is widely used to train teachers, interviewers, doctors and nurses, managers and supervisors, policemen, and for many other occupations which involve dealing with people. Those with effective social skills are more likely to be successful at work – their pupils learn more, their patients recover faster, their subordinates are happier and work harder, their speeches or lectures are better received, and they themselves are more successful. People with inadequate everyday social skills become anxious and depressed, may become patients, find it more difficult to get a job or more difficult to cooperate successfully with other people at work, and may lose their jobs.

Many people travel abroad, for holidays or work, or have to deal with members of other cultures in their own country. SST can help here, by discovering the gestures, rules, or other features of the other group's behaviour, and by finding the commonest sources of friction and showing how to avoid them.

SST is not always readily available. It can be given to patients if there is a trainer on the staff, and is often given to occupational groups, once a training scheme has been established. It is much less widely available to the general public, and I wish that it could be provided at leisure or adult education centres.

What is the best method of SST? In the past people learnt their social skills by doing them, on the job in the case of work skills. We now know that this is a slow and often ineffective method – people may never discover the best skills. Laboratory exercises are much more effective, especially role-playing with video feedback, though this needs to be supplemented by special exercises for particular aspects of social behaviour, and instruction in the principles of social behaviour. And there are some skills, such as those of the police, where it is difficult to reproduce in the lab the situations with which they will have to deal; an alternative is learning on the job, but coached by a tutor constable on the spot.

How successful is SST? For lonely and isolated people it may be the only way. For neurotic patients with social difficulties it is as good or better than the alternatives. For work skills it speeds things up, and may be the only way of dealing with some kinds of failure. For inter-cultural skills it is fast and effective. However it works best if the trainer has access to a good set of exercises and materials, and can tailor the training to the needs of the clients.

This book presents a wealth of new exercises and materials, that have been tried out, and found acceptable to trainees. Some of the main ideas which trainees need to grasp are clearly presented and supported by good illustrations. I hope that it will be widely used.

Michael Argyle
University of Oxford, 1991

PREFACE

The purpose of this book is to act as a compendium of ideas, none of them foolproof though all of them based on well-established therapeutic principles.

The visual format of the material is designed to highlight possible connections between ideas and to present a coherent, digestible whole. It is not intended as an over-simplification of often complex problems with a variety of possible solutions.

The ideas presented here should act as a stimulus to therapists and trainers working with clients who need to develop more effective social communication skills.

While this is not a recipe book, it is a collection of starting points with the emphasis on clients trying out skills for themselves in their community.

Long-stay institutions eg. psychiatric hospitals, hospitals for people with learning difficulties
Educational settings eg. adult learning institutes, colleges of further education
Residential settings eg. hostels, community group homes
Day care settings eg. day centres, day hospitals
Community settings eg. youth clubs, Manpower Services Commission (MSC) projects

Table 1 *Social communication: target groups*

HOW TO USE THIS BOOK

Sections 1 and 2 provide practical and theoretical information for therapists and group leaders wishing to know more about setting up and running social communication groups.

The activities in Sections 3 and 4 are presented in six groups, each colour coded for easy reference.

Whilst activities do not always fall neatly into distinct categories, these have been further divided into sections to show movement across activities, from observation skills to the transfer of skills to a community context.

Stage 1 – *Looking and Listening to Others*
Clients observe and identify particular social communication skills used by people around them.

Stage 2 – *Looking and Listening to Ourselves*
Clients identify their own skills and needs.

Stage 3 – *Try it Out*
New skills are tried out within the safe environment of the group.

Stage 4 – *Stepping Out*
Clients are supported in making any new skills part of their daily lives.

Activities are made progressively more challenging by extending the group's decision-making skills, and by providing a range of practice opportunities.

STEPPING OUT, NOT STAYING PUT

An important part of any social skills programme is to allow clients opportunities to practise relevant social communication skills in as realistic a context as possible. This develops the client's confidence and can ensure that the skills learned are retained and can become part of the client's repertoire of everyday communication skills.

The practical implication for group leaders is that it is clearly not possible to hold every session in the local shopping centre or nearby café. However, group leaders can make full use of relevant role-play scenarios and visits to appropriate community facilities. These experiences can act as a link between the comparative safety of the learning situation and the real life challenges of community living. It may also be possible to represent a wider social context, not only in terms of settings, but in terms of a variety of people who can become involved at different stages of a programme – other health professionals, volunteers, relatives and friends.

The process of transferring new skills from the learning situation to the community can be guided by the principles of generalization (*see Figure 1*).

The success of any social skills programme will depend on the ability of the group leader to encourage clients not to stay put but to step out into their own everyday communities with confidence.

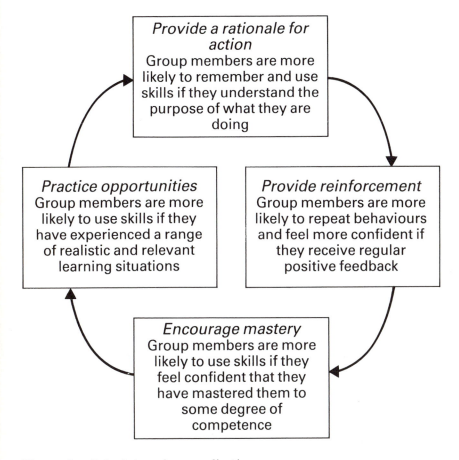

Figure 1 *Principles of generalization*

ACKNOWLEDGEMENTS

The authors would like to thank all colleagues, clients and students who have either been the catalysts or recipients of the ideas and activities presented in this book.

The book itself is also a tribute to effective social communication between the authors, who despite being in different places and being involved in other projects, worked together to produce the final text.

WHAT IS SOCIAL COMMUNICATION?

WHY DO WE NEED TO COMMUNICATE?

Three basic elements encourage our need to communicate (**Schutz**, 1988).

1 **Identity**
   Provides a sense of belonging to a certain group.
   Provides a feeling of involvement and acknowledgement.

2 **Control**
   Able to initiate action and respond to others.
   Able to determine to whom we speak and what we say.

3 **Acceptance**
   The desire to make friends and be liked.
   The desire to fit in and be accepted.

MAIN FEATURES OF SOCIAL COMMUNICATION

1 It is purposeful – aimed towards an intended goal, eg. short-term goal: asking someone in the street for directions; long-term goal: planning and organizing a holiday.

2 It can be determined – the individual can influence the when, who and how of interaction. For example making a telephone call and arranging a visit to a relative.

3 It is adaptable – different social communication skills are needed in different situations, and may vary according to interpersonal, environmental or cultural factors, eg. going to a party: *informal occasion* – sitting around in small groups and chatting, casual dress; *formal occasion* – being introduced to others by host or hostess, being smartly dressed.

4 It is co-ordinated – an effective interaction depends on the integration of body language and verbal language, eg. giving a compliment – in order to sound genuine, facial expression and posture need to match what is being said.

5 It can be improved – social communication skills can be developed through practice and positive reinforcement, eg. learning to make a telephone call, different stages can be identified and each stage practised as a separate step (**Hargie *et al***, 1981).

BODY LANGUAGE Non-verbal skills	SPOKEN LANGUAGE Verbal skills
Complements Illustrates what is being said	**Communicates** Conveys information, facts, opinions, feelings
Emphasizes Stresses words or phrases	**Clarifies** Nature of a relationship confirms status, roles of participants
Guides Indicates 'turn-taking' in conversation	**Guides** Socially accepted rules (norms) for conversation: when, what and how of conversation
Replaces Symbolic representation of the spoken word or phrases; ritualized routines are part of social convention	**Fulfils** Meets human need of wanting to be liked by others and to make friends

Table 1.1   *Purpose of social communication*

ACQUISITION OF SOCIAL COMMUNICATION SKILLS

Learning a new skill requires a helpful example to emulate, and opportunities to practise in a series of steps, with support and encouragement.

A focus on performance alone is often not sufficient to guarantee the achievement of long-term goals. It is important to engage the individual's desire to achieve and improve, and to take a more active control over their social environment.

The Stages of Skill Learning

1   **Demonstration:** *"This is how you do it. Watch me".*
   ▶ The demonstration should be carried out by a realistic role model (not necessarily an 'expert').

▶ It sets standards for the skilled performance and shows the client what it is possible to achieve.

▶ Learning is enhanced if the client is actively involved.

2 **Practice:** *"Now you have a go".*

▶ The skill is broken down into a series of steps.

▶ Allow repeated practice of key steps (components of the skill).

▶ Keep a focus on the complete skill so that learners remain clear about the end goal (sum of the components).

3 **Guidance:** *"Watch out for this. Be careful here".*

▶ Use cues to prompt a skilled performance (physical, visual and verbal clues).

▶ Guide the learner through the initial steps to reduce anxiety and fear of failing.

▶ Provide the opportunity to practice the complete skill several times unaided to ensure mastery.

4 **Feedback:** *"Well done. That was very good".*

▶ Praise from others, during practice or after completing the skill, aids recall.

▶ Feedback gives a sense of achievement and pride in completing a skill.

THEORETICAL PERSPECTIVES

Though there are many and various definitions of social skills, the parameters of social competence remain elusive.

Social competence is essentially a synthesis of skills, knowledge and attitudes, enabling an individual to adapt social performance to different contexts. The fact that this concept remains so difficult to pin down highlights the uniqueness of each individual's repertoire of skills and kaleidoscope of social experiences.

It would be unrealistic and undesirable to expect that we can be socially competent in every social situation. Variables such as the setting, the time of day and other people can significantly influence the way we respond.

An appreciation of the theoretical background to social communication can help group leaders to establish useful guiding principles, develop a rationale for action and enhance critical evaluation.

The overview presented here is a succinct guide to some relevant concepts and ideas that group leaders may find stimulating and worthy of further study.

Concept of Social Interest

The human desire to communicate with others is propelled by an innate social instinct. There is a need to identify collectively with others, and value is placed on the concept of 'community'.

Keysource: **Adler & Rodman** (1988) – individual psychology theory

Learning through Experience

Human behaviour is predominantly acquired by observing others and following their example. Through modelling, humans can benefit from the experience of others and acquire a new skill more quickly than by trial and error methods.

Humans can isolate key principles from one skill and apply them to another novel and self-initiated situation.

Keysource: **Argyle** (1987) – social skills model

Recognition Hunger

Humans are essentially driven by a need to be acknowledged by others and this is satisfied by either physical recognition (body language such as touch) or psychological recognition (verbal language such as giving a compliment).

Individuals have the potential to fully influence their responses in social situations.

Keysource: **Berne** (1975) – transactional analysis

Hierarchy of Needs

The hierarchial representation of needs places physiological and safety needs as being more 'potent' (basic and over-riding) than belongingness and esteem needs.

Humans, as individuals, have the capacity for self-development and for achieving their full potential (self-actualization).

Keysource: **Maslow** (1987) – theory of human motivation

SUMMARY: KEY POINTS

▶ To belong to and relate to others is a fundamental human need;

▶ The acquisition of skills is influenced by the example of others;

▶ Motivation is an important stimulus for initiating action;

▶ Feedback is an important stimulus for learning to progress and retaining what is learned.

GUIDELINES FOR SETTING UP AND RUNNING GROUPS

WHY SOCIAL COMMUNICATION GROUPS?

The advantages of group work:
- ▶ Ready-made social context;
- ▶ Provides peer-group support;
- ▶ Offers a variety of role models;
- ▶ Facilitates immediate use of skills;
- ▶ Powerful source of feedback and reinforcement;
- ▶ Effective use of resources and facilities;
- ▶ Optimum group size between five and 12 group members;
- ▶ Small groups can help build up trust and co-operation between participants.

STAGES OF GROUP DEVELOPMENT (TUCKMAN, 1981)

Tuckman's five stages of group development recognize that the running of a group consists not only of the content of the sessions, but also that the group itself evolves over time.

Though not a definitive guide to group processes, Tuckman's stages are a useful framework which can help to highlight key issues to be addressed by group leaders.

As a group leader, the process of working collaboratively in a group may be familiar territory, but new group members may be preoccupied with uncertainties.

The following checklist uses Tuckman's stages of group development as a pathway through these concerns, and raises content and process issues for the group leader to consider.

Stage One: Forming

Group concerns
- ▶ What shall we do?
- ▶ Why should we do it?
- ▶ Anxiety, uncertainty, vulnerability;
- ▶ Reliance on group leader.

Group leader objectives
- ▶ To explain purpose of group;

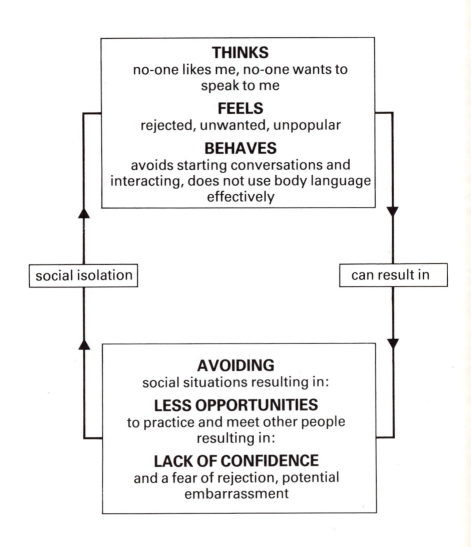

Figure 2.1   *The social isolation cycle*

▶ To reassure, be supportive;

▶ To acknowledge apprehension and fears.

Group leader tasks

1 Identify a selection criteria for the group.
2 Select appropriate assessment methods in order to establish individual and group baselines of behaviour. Examples are:
   a) *In vivo* observation (based in the everyday setting, informal).
   b) Use of observational checklists, rating scales and self-monitoring techniques.
   c) Liaising with staff, family and friends and other health care workers.
   d) One-to-one interview to clarify the individual's perception of their own social communication needs.
   e) Role-play enactments.
3 Decide on the design of the social communication programme:
   Structured approach: Set sequence of skills from body language to verbal language allows for recapping, reinforcement of basic skills. Appropriate for larger groups, of a fixed and constant membership.
   Semi-structured approach: Starts with a 'top-up' on basic skills, leads on to focus on individual needs.
   Unstructured approach: Often variable membership, more open format possible. Appropriate for smaller groups to focus on individual needs, working on selected skills only.
4 Plan the first session:
   ▶ Check venue for facilities: comfortable room, privacy, available refreshments, toilets.
   ▶ Teamwork strategy: discuss and clarify roles of group leader and co-leader.
   ▶ Provide clear starting instructions for the group members: when? where? with whom?
   ▶ Group introductions and 'getting to know you' activities.
   ▶ Acknowledge each individual member (eye contact, use of name).
   ▶ Outline programme and explain contents.
   ▶ Clarify group rules (attendance, any shared responsibilities).
   ▶ Allay anxieties, providing reassurance.
   ▶ Encourage active participation: use of warm-up activities as a tension-reducer.

► Ensure that each individual has made contact with at least two or three other members in the group.

Stage Two: Storming

Group concerns
► How can it be done?
► Differences of opinion expressed;
► Conflict between members, about task.

Group leader objectives
► To establish limits;
► To clarify and respond to individual needs.

Group leader tasks
1   Select the most appropriate learning methods for the group:
   a) Explanation: establish a rationale for skill acquisition.
   b) Modelling/demonstration: use group leaders, other group members or video extracts (demonstrating realistic and achievable social communication).
   c) Role-play/enactment: needs clear guidelines and instructions for successful outcome. Use everyday situations relevant to the group.
2   Clarify the role of group members and of group leaders.

Stage Three: Norming

Group concerns
► We can do it!
► Beginnings of group co-operation;
► Building up a network of mutual support;
► Familiarity and trust.

Group leader objectives
► To foster group cohesion;
► To link ideas and wishes to action;
► To keep targets achievable and realistic.

Group leader tasks

1 Facilitate group cohesion:
   a) Provide feedback and encouragement for specific contributions: acknowledging attempting a task as well as its successful completion.
   b) Maintain a positive outlook: focus on the group's assets and present abilities.
   c) Deal with issues such as erratic attendance, conflicts between individual members as they arise.
   d) Plan definite beginnings and endings to each session, fostering a constructive atmosphere.
2 Facilitate group co-operation:
   a) Emphasize active participation: plenty of doing!
   b) Acknowledge all group members, though levels of participation may vary.
   c) Be prepared to repeat explanations and instructions and to modify activities to meet the abilities of the group.
   d) Use a variety of learning methods and do not stick to the same format every session; familiarity can breed . . . boredom!

Stage Four: Performing

Group concerns
▶ We are doing it!
▶ Contributing towards group goals;
▶ Commitment to group – members and task.

Group leader objectives
▶ To encourage participation;
▶ To facilitate productive problem solving;
▶ To remain flexible and responsive to individual needs.

Group leader tasks
1 Use linking experiences to encourage use of skills in a wider social context (visits, use of facilities in the community).
2 Encourage the generalization of skills:
   a) Pitch activities at the appropriate level for the group.
   b) Clarify the relevance of skills to group members' everyday life.

c) Use of specific homework tasks between sessions giving clear guidelines as to what? when? how? with whom?
d) Recapping on main points from previous sessions, highlighting progress to date.

Stage Five: Ending

Group concerns
▶ Have we achieved our targets?
▶ Reluctance to end the sessions;
▶ Dependence on group support and social contact.

Group leader objectives
▶ To allow individuals to leave;
▶ To maintain group cohesion and commitment;
▶ To facilitate ending on a positive, constructive note.

Group leader tasks
1 Identify appropriate ways of evaluating the outcome:
   a) Re-assessment;
   b) Feedback from family and relatives, staff and other group members.
   c) Achievement of clearly specified targets.
2 Identify appropriate methods of follow-up:
   a) Identify a contact person/link worker;
   b) Provide a follow-up review session;
   c) Provide a refresher 'top up' course.
3 Incorporate methods that will enhance the continued use of skills:
   a) Use of linking experiences (relevant and realistic role-plays, variety of people involved).
   b) Provide plenty of practice opportunities (warm-ups and activities, role-play, homework tasks).
   c) Include adequate repetition and reinforcement of main principles, stressing important 'tips for success'.
   d) Ensure that group members appreciate the usefulness of social communication in the community, and have understood the 'why' not just the 'how'.

SUMMARY

	BASIC SKILLS LEVEL	COMPLEX SKILLS LEVEL
Identifying specific problems	Limited repertoire of skills due to: ▶ faulty or impeded social learning; ▶ lack of opportunities to socialize; ▶ lack of appropriate role models.	Has an established basic repertoire of skills but: ▶ lacks confidence in particular skills; ▶ anxious in social situations; ▶ insufficient positive reinforcement and practice opportunities.
Characteristics of programme	Initial stages of programme require frequent repetition and reinforcement of main points.	Individualized programmes more feasible, pitched at needs identified by group members.
Concentration span	Short sessions of 30 to 45 minutes. Longer sessions can incorporate tea breaks or other breaks.	Sessions of longer duration: one to two hours.
Time span	Programme may extend over a period of time – a number of weeks, months. Revision or top-up sessions may be necessary.	Intensive programme of a short series of sessions, or a workshop format may be possible.

Table 2.1 *Summary*

	BASIC SKILLS LEVEL	COMPLEX SKILLS LEVEL
Types of activities/ exercises	Programme can include a range of appropriate activities/games: ▶ avoids getting stuck and group members losing interest; ▶ targeted at an achievable level.	A variety of learning methods can be used: ▶ role-play ▶ discussion groups ▶ video feedback ▶ problem-solving tasks.
Feedback and reinforcement	Feedback and encouragement from group leader and other group members important for sustaining motivation. Progress and consolidation may be very gradual, therefore reinforcement over time is essential.	Self-reinforcement to be encouraged: individual members can learn to monitor and appreciate their own progress.
Support	Establish a receptive, non-judgemental group environment. Encourage liaison with ward staff, other health professionals, relatives and friends.	Group members may continue to provide support for each other outside sessions, eg. telephone numbers and facilitating 'link-ups'.

Table 2.1 *Summary* (cont.)

BASIC SOCIAL COMMUNICATION

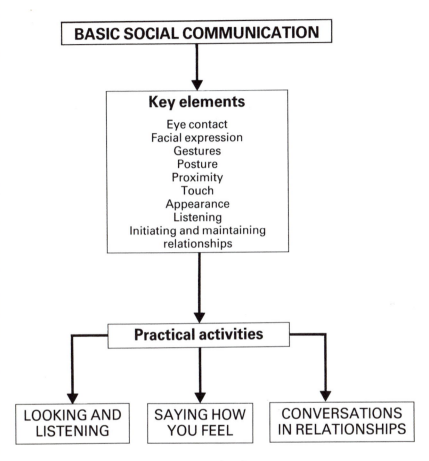

Figure 3.1 *Basic social communication*

WHAT ARE BASIC SOCIAL COMMUNICATION SKILLS?

Basic social communication skills are the everyday 'bread and butter' behaviours that enable an individual to get along socially with other people.

They provide the essential framework of skills that can be developed over time with regular practice. Individuals can progress to more complex skills, but unless the basic skills are understood and used, further refinement will be difficult to achieve.

Though social skills bases its principles and methods on behavioural psychology, it is important to remember that relating to people cannot be reduced to a purely scientific formula. Effective social skills is also about alerting group members to the hidden 'nooks and crannies' of interaction. Like learning the rules of grammar, there are always exceptions to the rules and particular social situations that demand unique responses.

EYE CONTACT

CHARACTERISTICS

1 Mutual eye gaze – signals interest and a willingness to interact further (lasts approximately one second).

2 Appropriate eye contact between two strangers follows this pattern:
- Brief eye contact;
- Look briefly away;
- Eye contact again;
- Establishes either a **positive** response (can progress further, may initiate a conversation) or a **negative** response (uninterest, avoiding interaction).

TOO MUCH

Prolonged intense eye contact is characterized by a staring, fixed gaze. It may be interpreted as being impolite and rude, particularly amongst strangers or acquaintances. Use of fixed eye contact if angry can be confrontative and aggressive.

TOO LITTLE

Reduced eye contact may appear as:

a) Excessive blinking or attempting to cover eyes with hands.

b) Avoiding eye contact by averting gaze, looking down or away. It may be interpreted as being due to anxiety or shyness and a reluctance to make contact and interact. It can be perceived as being insincere and having 'something to hide' (not being able to look someone in the face).

TARGET

Good eye contact helps to guide the pace and co-ordination of a conversation. It produces useful handover cues, indicating 'turns' in a conversation. Looking away when you have finished talking (often done automatically) signals that it is the other person's turn to speak.

FACIAL EXPRESSION

CHARACTERISTICS

1   Researchers have identified eight distinct positions of the eye-brows, eight positions of the eyes and ten positions of the lower face.

2   Six primary facial expressions have been identified:
  ▶ anger
  ▶ fear
  ▶ disgust
  ▶ happiness
  ▶ sadness
  ▶ surprise

TOO MUCH

Exaggerated facial expressions may be inappropriate for the social occasion (formal situation). They may convey too much personal information too soon (sadness or happiness) and this may embarrass a newly-made acquaintance or friend.

Excessive use of facial expressions can be perceived as being insincere and contrived and may distract from what is actually being said.

TOO LITTLE

A blank, expressionless face, conveying no emotional response to the situation, can be perceived as appearing impersonal, aloof, and lacking in emotional warmth.

A lack of facial expression provides no feedback to another person as to whether interactions are on the same wavelength.

TARGET

1   Appropriate smiling (involving the whole face, not just upturning the corners of the mouth) provides positive feedback – 'I like you, please continue!'

2   Facial expressions match the emotional tone of the conversation or situation (looking happy at a party, looking frightened in a horror film).

GESTURES

CHARACTERISTICS

1 Gesture can be intentional (adding emphasis to language) or unintentional (may 'leak' emotional state).
2 Gestures include such movements as head nods, fist-making, rubbing of hands (involving head or hands).

TOO MUCH

1 Inappropriate gestures may not match what is being said and give out mixed, confusing messages.
2 Excessive gesturing (vigorous head nodding, flailing arms) may distract from what is being said.

3   Gestures can be misunderstood due to cultural variations: a simple gesture of greeting in one culture may be an offensive sign in another.

TOO LITTLE

1   Excessive fidgeting can be distracting and may signal a person's unease and anxiety as may nervous habits such as nail biting, scratching and fiddling with hair.
2   Lack of appropriate gestures (ritualized routines such as waving goodbye) may be perceived as being uninterested and unwilling to respond.

TARGET

Gesture provides interest to what is being said, it adds 'colourful' flourishes and illustrations. Appropriate use of gesture helps to guide the pace of conversation and add emotional emphasis to it (stamping foot when angry).

CHARACTERISTICS

1 There are two main postural positions – tension and relaxation.
2 Posture cues (tense or relaxed posture) convey the nature of relationships within social interaction (eg. pupil going to see the head teacher).

TOO MUCH

A very tense posture conveys anxiety and apprehension (eg. sitting on the edge of the chair; stiff, upright posture; tense muscles). It may also make others feel uncomfortable and nervous.

Inappropriate posture in formal situations may give the wrong impression, for instance a very relaxed posture in a job interview may be perceived as being indifferent or over-confident.

TOO LITTLE

A listless posture (drooping shoulders, slouching, head bowed) can be perceived as withdrawn, insular behaviour. It may convey boredom or apathy and may not provide any encouraging positive feedback to others.

TARGET

1   An open, confident and alert posture indicates a willingness to be approached and to be communicative.
2   It enables face-to-face interaction to take place, with face, gaze and body positioned towards the other person.

PROXIMITY

CHARACTERISTICS

1 The use of personal space acts as a 'buffer zone' in social situations.
2 Defines a person's 'territory'.
    a) Intimate distance (up to 18 inches)
       ▶ Intimate personal space;
       ▶ Sharing involves trust, and a willingness to be intimate.
    b) Personal distance (18 inches to four feet)
       ▶ Everyday social encounters;
       ▶ Appropriate for casual conversations.

c) Social distance (four feet to 12 feet)
   ▶ Formal encounters (at work);
   ▶ More impersonal everyday encounters.
d) Public distance (12 feet and beyond)
   Ranges from distance between teacher and pupils to distance between actors and an audience.

TOO MUCH

Disregarding someone's personal space can be perceived as being 'pushy' and an invasion of their privacy. Moving in too close, too soon when meeting someone for the first time may cause embarrassment and unease.

TOO LITTLE

Use of physical objects to act as a barrier to prevent closer contact (eg. sitting behind a desk).

TARGET

Closer proximity is appropriate as a relationship develops (from social to intimate distance).

TOUCH

CHARACTERISTICS

1 Neutral body contact – occurs within professional relationships (eg. between doctor and patient) and within more formal social relationships (eg. shaking hands at the beginning of a job interview).

2 Active body contact – occurs within more personal and intimate relationships (eg. between mother and child, husband and wife), it conveys concern and shared trust.

TOO MUCH

1 Active body contact in more formal social occasions can cause embarrassment or may be interpreted as being very forward and over-familiar.

2 Active or neutral use of touch varies from culture to culture, and again can be a source of misunderstanding or misinterpretation.

TOO LITTLE

A lack of spontaneous touch can be perceived as being rather cold and unfeeling in certain situations such as comforting or congratulating a friend.

TARGET

Appropriate use of touch in everyday situations such as greetings, farewells, congratulating and guiding (eg. taking an elderly person's arm to help them across the road).

APPEARANCE

CHARACTERISTICS

1. Style and manner of dress may reflect age, sex, status, personality and occupation.
2. Choice of clothes expresses a person's individuality and may convey mood.

TOO MUCH

Inappropriate choice of dress (not 'dressing the part') can result in being ignored and feeling left out (eg. wearing casual clothes at a formal reception).

Similarly extremes of dress may be distracting and divert attention away from what is being said.

TOO LITTLE

A neglected personal appearance may be perceived as being uninterested in creating a good impression (unkempt hair, untidy, dirty clothes).

Not looking 'presentable' for the occasion or season may result in being avoided by others.

TARGET

1   The primary effect – personal appearance does have a lot of impact when forming initial first impressions.
2   'Dressing the part' conveys a willingness to 'fit in' and be involved with others.

LISTENING

CHARACTERISTICS

1 Hearing: the physiological aspects of listening.
2 Attending: a selective process, giving meaning to what is heard.
3 Understanding: interpreting what is heard, with reference to previous knowledge, social context and rules of grammar.
4 Remembering: the residual message.

TOO MUCH

Selective listening (only listening to parts of a conversation) can result in misunderstanding, jumping to conclusions and making assumptions.

TOO LITTLE

A distracting environment may impede effective listening (eg. a stuffy room, loud music, traffic noise).

Lack of sustained effort and concentration may result in missing the full sense of what is being said.

TARGET

1 The effective listener is attentive and gives positive reinforcement by for example maintaining eye contact, smiling, nodding in agreement.

2 Attention can be conveyed by appropriate body language such as a relaxed posture and appropriate facial expression.

3 Being aware of the other person's body language, what is being said and the way it is being said, can give important cues.

CHARACTERISTICS

1 Getting started involves stages of 'coming together':
   a) exploration (establishing common ground);
   b) acceptance (developing trust and understanding);
   c) compatibility (increased closeness and sharing).
2 We tend to develop friendships with those whom we meet often and can easily identify with.

TOO MUCH

There needs to be a mutual desire to develop a relationship and become friends. Being too eager and trying to rush the friendship (closeness and sharing before establishing common ground) may be over-whelming and alarming for others.

TOO LITTLE

Failing to take the initiative in starting a relationship may be due to a fear of taking risks and being rejected. This may result in opportunities for developing friendships being missed.

TARGET

1 A starting point may be a shared interest or a common experience.

2 Small talk initially helps to 'break the ice' and establish a comfortable atmosphere, appropriate topics include:

   a) holidays

   b) interests/hobbies

   c) news items

   d) funny incidents

   e) the weather

   f) personal acknowledgement (a compliment)

CHARACTERISTICS

1   A newly formed friendship involves social recognition both informally – "You two seem to be good friends" and formally – becoming business partners.

2   'Friendships are usually based on being physically close; being involved in mutual activities; similar attitudes, values, background, personality and interests, expressing mutual liking' (**Zimbardo**, 1986).

TOO MUCH

The pace of a developing relationship can be rushed by making too many demands or making assumptions.

Being possessive or jealous does not allow each individual to develop a network of different types of relationships at different levels of closeness.

TOO LITTLE

Failure to conclude a meeting on a positive, forward-looking note may result in a friendship losing its impetus and fizzling out. Similarly ending conversations in a hesitant or abrupt manner may convey a lack of interest – closures are just as important as openings.

TARGET

1   To maintain a balance between closeness and sharing and to allow individual differences.
2   A friendship needs a degree of committment and a willingness to continue if it is to develop, for example being there for a friend if in need.

SELF-DISCLOSURE

CHARACTERISTICS

1   Self-disclosure involves the exchange of facts, opinions or feelings.
2   It is the act of deliberately revealing significant information about yourself, usually to one other person.
3   Women more readily self-disclose than men.

TOO MUCH

Revealing intimate details very early on in a conversation can cause embarrassment and may overwhelm the listener.

Frequent self-disclosure may be perceived as being insincere and trite and may not be taken seriously.

TOO LITTLE

A reluctance to share personal information may convey lack of trust in the listener. Similarly self-disclosures, unless reciprocated, may inhibit the development of a conversation (keeping to safer, less personal subjects).

TARGET

1   Self-disclosure provides the opportunity to discover common ground (shared interests and experiences past or present).
2   Mutual self-disclosure helps to develop trust and encourages open and more personal communication.

EMPATHY

CHARACTERISTICS

1 The ability to see the world from another person's point of view – 'taking the role of the other'.

2 We can empathize more readily with people who are similar to ourselves – in terms of age, sex, social background, intelligence or culture.

TOO MUCH

Empathy involves seeing the situation from the other person's point of view instead of being judgemental and moralistic.

An empathetic response is prevented by becoming immersed in your own feelings and not responding to someone else's needs.

TOO LITTLE

Lack of appropriate empathetic responses can be interpreted as being thoughtless and uncaring, for instance, when a friend is talking about a recent loss. In addition a general lack of sensitivity and awareness may mean that cues of how someone really feels about a situation/event are not picked up (eg. noticing body language).

TARGET

1   A sincere regard for others and a genuine desire to appreciate the other person's viewpoint.
2   The ability to facilitate a more open and trusting relationship.

POSITIVE REGARD

CHARACTERISTICS

1 We tend to seek out people who give us positive feedback and 'rewards' (eg. acknowledgement, praise, compliments).
2 'Rewarding' qualities include:
   a) a cheerful attitude;
   b) a helpful manner;
   c) friendly tone of voice;
   d) approachable and attentive posture;
   e) providing feedback (smiling, agreement, making appropriate comments).

TOO MUCH

Being deliberately nice to others in order to win approval or gain favours shows insincerity rather than positive regard. Positive feedback needs to be built upon and consistent – being friendly one moment and aloof the next will confuse people and inhibit friendships from developing.

TOO LITTLE

The term 'socially bankrupt' (**Longabough et al**, 1969) refers to the absence of rewarding qualities and the inability to give in a friendship: rewarding qualities do need to be reciprocated. In some cases anxiety or shyness may prevent someone giving and receiving positive feedback appropriately.

TARGET

1 Positive regard conveys a feeling of being worth getting to know and that you matter.
2 Giving positive feedback to others can lead to a widening social circle and the opportunity to make more friends.

SUMMARY OF TARGET BEHAVIOURS

Body language

1   An open posture, indicating a willingness to be approached.
2   The ability to maintain appropriate eye contact.
3   The use of animated and relevant gestures.
4   A sensitive and responsive use of physical contact.
5   An appropriate use of positive feedback (eg. smiles, nods).
6   The use of handover cues in conversation (let the other person have a turn in speaking).

Verbal language

1   A genuine, friendly manner including tone of voice and facial expression.
2   The ability to share personal details in an appropriate manner.
3   A smooth pattern of interaction – not interrupting, few awkward silences, clear and unambiguous communication.
4   Complementary body language: what is being said matches how it is being said.

Towards stepping out

The ability to respond to social situations utilizing the following skills:

1   Can adapt to meet the requirements of different social situations (formal and informal).
2   Willing to take risks occasionally and take the initiative in starting conversations.
3   Has a repertoire of face-saving ploys to avoid embarrassing moments (eg. making a joke, giving an apology, or able to change the topic of conversation).
4   Feels socially confident: enjoys mixing socially for its own sake, and is not over-dependent on the feedback and approval of others.
5   Has opportunities to practise and try out using initiative and responding to others in a range of different social situations.

PRACTICAL ACTIVITIES

LOOKING AND LISTENING

Aims
1 To increase group members' awareness of the people, places and customs that make up their particular community.
2 To encourage group members to identify their own individual style of communicating.

List of practical activities
Looking and Listening to Others
Descriptions/51
Who is It?/52
Guess the Job/53
Witness/54
Looking and Listening to Ourselves
Look at Yourself/55
Describe Yourself/56
Listen to Yourself/57
Spot the Change/58
Try it Out
Have a Go!/59
Copy Cats/60
Taste that Smell!/61
Hobbies/62

DESCRIPTIONS

MATERIALS

Photographs of people from magazines, newspapers and supplements. Flip chart and pens.

PROCEDURE

The group leader presents a selection of photographs. All players take it in turn to describe in detail what they see.

A basic framework for the descriptions may be helpful, as in the one below. Additional descriptive categories could be added such as:

▶ occupation

▶ type of car

▶ favourite holiday destination

▶ family and friends

▶ hobbies

▶ name

People can then take it in turns to describe one of the photographs on view until the rest of the group can guess who they are talking about. The more similar the photographs, the more challenging the activity.

DESCRIPTIONS
Sex
Age
Build
Height
Eye colour
Hair colour
Nationality
Dress
Any unusual features

Figure 3.2 *Descriptions*

WHO IS IT?

MATERIALS

Photographs of people relevant to the group, eg. residential staff, television personalities, family members. Samples of the same people talking on tape.

PROCEDURE

The group leader presents the photographs for people to identify. This activity can be made more challenging by blanking out the eyes in a photograph (*see Figure 3.3*).

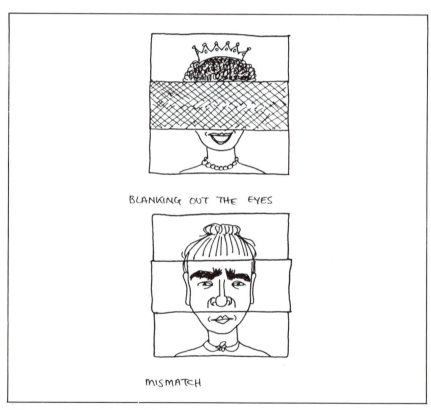

BLANKING OUT THE EYES

MISMATCH

Figure 3.3 *Who is it?*

The group leader plays the taped voice samples for people to guess who is talking.

GUESS THE JOB

MATERIALS

Photographs or pictures of people in the community in their work environment.

PROCEDURE

The group leader shows the photographs and the group has to identify their occupation in the community.

WITNESS

MATERIALS

Video recording of an acted scene involving three to four people or a section of a television programme or film.

PROCEDURE

The group leader shows a few seconds/minutes of film of an action scene, for example a hold-up.

The video is then switched off, group members act as witnesses and describe some of the people seen.

This activity can be organized individually, in pairs or small groups. The video can be re-run as often as people wish, in order to check their descriptions.

LOOK AT YOURSELF

MATERIALS

Polaroid camera or video camera if appropriate.

PROCEDURE

People are encouraged to take photographs of each other in different poses, for example, standing, laughing or in profile.

It is possible to set some cameras up so that people can take self-portraits and this may be preferred by some. If the group feels ready to use the video camera, this can be used as another means of encouraging everyone to feel comfortable looking at themselves.

Participants may wish to keep the photographs of themselves.

DESCRIBE YOURSELF

MATERIALS

Photographs and video recordings from *Look at Yourself* if required.

PROCEDURE

People take it in turn to describe themselves to the group in whatever way they wish. A basic framework may be helpful (*see Descriptions p.51*). The photographs may be used as cues for people when giving their description.

LISTEN TO YOURSELF

MATERIALS

A tape recorder with microphone.

PROCEDURE

Each person is encouraged to speak on tape and become familiar with hearing their own voice. After each person has had a turn, the tapes can be played for the group to guess the identity of each speaker.

SPOT THE CHANGE

MATERIALS

A few clothes props may be useful, such as glasses, jewellery, scarves.

PROCEDURE

Participants take it in turns to go out of the room and change three things about themselves, for example, remove a watch, put on a tie and roll-up their sleeves. The rest of the group have to decide what has been changed when the person comes back into the room.

HAVE A GO!

MATERIALS

Mirrors, make-up, jewellery, hats, ties, wigs, glasses, high heels, and anything else available, polaroid camera.

PROCEDURE

Everyone is given time and privacy, where necessary, to experiment with changing their appearance or just trying out what is available to see how it looks, for example wearing nail varnish or a tie.

Photographs can be taken if people choose.

COPY CATS

MATERIALS

Varied clothes props, uniforms, make-up.

PROCEDURE

People take turns to impersonate someone they know, with or without props. Each person chooses how they will do their impersonation.

TASTE THAT SMELL!

MATERIALS

1   Tastes – a selection of foods available in the client's community, eg. sweet and sour pork, curry, mangoes, poppadums, melon.
2   Smells – a variety of toiletries for men and women, eg. shower gel, talcum powder, perfume, aftershave, soaps with different scents.

PROCEDURE

The group leader will need to collect together the various items for a tasting or smelling session. All the items are presented for the clients to sample and choose their likes and dislikes.

This activity will be most relevant where the items presented are readily available and visible in the client's local community.

Once clients have made various choices, this could be followed up by enabling them to influence meal-planning at home and by choosing favourite toiletries when shopping.

HOBBIES

MATERIALS

A wide selection of hobby materials; pictures, photographs, videos, books.

PROCEDURE

The group leader presents various materials of different hobbies that clients can try out. Or clients may prefer to go around local community centres to see what is available.

Visitors could be invited to the group to demonstrate a hobby, eg. jewellery making, photography, collecting.

WHAT DO I SEE?

MATERIALS

Photographs or videos from previous activities; paper and pens.

PROCEDURE

Each person is encouraged to notice their own appearance and presentation, likes and dislikes. A basic framework of description may be helpful, for example:

▶ dress sense

▶ tidiness

▶ posture

▶ voice

Participants can note their own observations in terms of strengths and needs. Here are two examples:

a) I always look smart (strength);

b) My voice is too quiet (need).

WHAT DO YOU SEE?

MATERIALS

Paper and pens.

PROCEDURE

The group leader asks everyone in the group to give some feedback to each other about their appearance and presentation. Everyone in the group should have a turn to say:

a)   "One thing I like about your appearance is . . ."

b)   "One thing I think you could improve is . . ."

The group leader may need to keep a firm grip on this activity to maintain a balance of strengths and needs.

CHANGES

MATERIALS

Paper and pens.

PROCEDURE

As a result of the previous activities, people may wish to make a change in their appearance and presentation.

This could be made as an agreement or pledge for change. For example:

1 To get my hair cut regularly;
2 To buy new shoes.

The rest of the group can offer support to each other and follow this through over future sessions.

FOLLOW-ON

MATERIALS

Information on local resources.

PROCEDURE

Resources in the community which would offer more information to group members on appearance and presentation could be contacted to follow up personal interests. The following suggestions may be useful to the group:

1   College of Further Education courses in health care and beauty.
2   A visit from a make-up or jewellery consultant.
3   Arrange a visit to a clothes store, possibly in the evening after hours.
4   Designer clothes for the disabled, where appropriate.

SAYING HOW YOU FEEL

Aims
1 To develop group members' skill in identifying and naming emotions.
2 To encourage expression of feelings.

List of practical activities

WHAT IS A FEELING?

MATERIALS

Photographs or sketches of a face showing each of the six most common expressions: surprise; anger; disgust; fear; happiness; and sadness (*see p. 70*). Flip chart, pens, paper, prepared voice tape, varied photographs showing posture and gesture of people.

PROCEDURE

Before going on to later activities, the group needs to agree a vocabulary to describe feelings.

The six basic expressions of:

▶ Anger
▶ Fear
▶ Disgust
▶ Happiness
▶ Sadness
▶ Surprise

need to be recognized by everyone. This vocabulary can be expanded in any way the group wants.

Using the voice tapes, facial expression photographs/sketches and other photographs, each person has a turn at recognizing how the six basic feelings are expressed through:

a) Facial expression
b) Posture
c) Gesture
d) Voice
e) Appearance
    Demonstration by the group leader may be helpful.

Figure 3.4   *What is a feeling?*

LOOK, HOW DO THEY FEEL?

MATERIALS

A variety of photographs, slides, and cartoons, showing people expressing different emotions. A videotape of film dramas.

PROCEDURE

People take turns to describe the pictures in terms of the framework given in the activity *Descriptions (see p.51)*.

The group leader may encourage people to choose one word which best describes the picture, eg. 'Happy'. Then ask "How do you know he is happy?" encouraging responses like "Because he's smiling, he is clapping his hands, he's relaxed, having a good laugh".

Video tapes can be played with NO sound so that the group can concentrate on watching how people express their feelings.

LISTEN, HOW DO THEY FEEL?

MATERIALS

Prepared voice tapes of the same message spoken in neutral, happy, sad, angry and frightened voices. Foreign language tapes, radio dramas.

PROCEDURE

People take turns to describe the feelings of the voices they hear. The group can discuss this together and reach an agreement.

PUTTING IT ALL TOGETHER

MATERIALS

Videotape of television and film dramas, and news items.

PROCEDURE

A selected videotape is played. The group then discuss what they observed, concentrating on who was feeling what and why, using the basic framework (*see Descriptions p.51*) where necessary.

HOW WOULD YOU FEEL IF ...?

MATERIALS

The group leader needs to have a collection of newspaper stories such as the following clip:

> Today a three year old boy was badly bitten by a dog while he was playing in the park.

PROCEDURE

Group members have turns at listening to an account and saying how they would feel if they were that person or their relative or friend. For example;

▶ How would you feel if you were the boy's parents?

▶ What could you do?

The idea of what they could do can also be introduced, although this is not the main emphasis at this stage. People can express how they feel either by talking, writing it down, or by drawing a picture.

SOAP BOX

MATERIALS

Six sheets of flip-chart paper, pens.

PROCEDURE

The group leader lays out six sheets and in the centre of each one writes one of the six basic feelings, eg.

> **anger**

Everyone brainstorms quickly the kind of things that make them angry and these are written on the chart. Examples may be things like:

▶ Waiting in queues
▶ Low pay
▶ Smoking in public

This exercise is repeated for each of the other five feelings.

1 Fear
2 Disgust
3 Happiness
4 Sadness
5 Surprise

SHARE YOUR FEELINGS

MATERIALS

None.

PROCEDURE

Taking the six basic feelings in turn, each person thinks of a time when they felt surprised, sad, and so on.

People share their accounts. Some may prefer to do this in pairs or small groups before talking to the main group. The group leader may need to provide cues such as "How did you feel on your first day at the day centre?"

SHOW YOUR FEELINGS

MATERIALS

Polaroid camera, film, video, tape-recorder, mirrors.

PROCEDURE

Everyone has a go at expressing each of the six basic feelings by:

a) facial expression
b) posture
c) gesture
d) voice

in front of the mirror and then having a photograph taken. Again, participants may want to keep a set of photographs.

PASS A FEELING

MATERIALS

Bean-bag or ball.

PROCEDURE

Everyone sits in a circle and throws a ball to each other. As someone catches the ball, the thrower calls out one of the six basic feelings which the catcher then acts out.

HIGH DRAMA

MATERIALS

Prepared short dramas for two people plus relevant props.

PROCEDURE

The group leader has a list of short dramatic scenes for two people to act out. Participants get together in groups and decide which person they will be and then act the scene.

These scenes should be short but dramatic, for example:

a)   Sheila is in a shop and accidentally knocks over an ornament. It crashes to the floor and breaks. The assistant walks over . . .

What happens next?

b)   Bill rings up a friend to say he has two free tickets to the Wembley Cup Final.

How does the conversation go?

MOOD MUSIC

MATERIALS

Tape recordings or records of varied music likely to be associated with feelings/mood such as Fleetwood Mac's *Albatross* or Elgar's *Pomp and Circumstance*.

PROCEDURE

Extracts of music are played and people are encouraged to express their responses. They may choose to say how they feel, mime, draw a picture or make a sculpture.

MOOD PICTURES

MATERIALS

Art books, posters or postcards of paintings.

PROCEDURE

Look at famous art paintings and discuss how they make people feel. The group leader may ask questions such as "What mood does this picture suggest?" Here are some examples of paintings that might be used:

Constable *The Haywain*

Turner *Snowstorm: Steamboat off a Harbour Mouth*

Degas *Dancers on a Stage*

Seurat *The Bathers: Asnives*

Van Gogh *Cornfield with Cypress*

Picasso *Weeping Woman*

Clients can select the picture that gives them most pleasure. This could be followed up by enabling the client to buy postcards or posters of their favourite pictures to decorate their rooms.

FEELINGS

MATERIALS

Pens and paper.

PROCEDURE

Each person is encouraged to think about their own feelings and the way they express them – are there any changes they want to make?

People could share their ideas on changes in pairs or groups. Any changes could be followed up in future sessions, for example, "If I am feeling fed up I will tell people from now on".

DIARY

MATERIALS

Pens and paper or booklets.

PROCEDURE

Each person is to keep a diary of how they felt every day between this session and the next time the group meets. The diaries can be written or use a relevant symbol system such as Rebus where appropriate.

At least one feeling and a reason for the feeling should be noted for each day. For example: *Wednesday* – surprise phone call from my cousin which really cheered me up.

A NIGHT OUT

MATERIALS

Entertainments information from the local paper, posters from theatres and cinemas.

PROCEDURE

The group leader presents the information about locally available entertainment.

The group discuss how they would feel about going to the different events. Examples are:

a) a horror film at the cinema;

b) folk-singing at the local pub;

c) a comedy play at the theatre;

d) prize night at the bingo hall.

Participants choose which entertainment they would like to go to. This could be followed up by enabling them to visit their chosen venue.

WHAT'S AVAILABLE?

MATERIALS

Information on local resources.

PROCEDURE

The group leader presents information about local resources which people may wish to follow up such as:

▶ amateur dramatics

▶ drama workshops

▶ relaxation groups

▶ yoga

▶ music, art, pottery classes

▶ sports

▶ entertainment

CONVERSATION IN RELATIONSHIPS

Aims
1 To explore what makes up a relationship and what kind of relationships people have.
2 To look at the language we use in order to establish and maintain relationships.

List of practical activities

WHAT IS A RELATIONSHIP?

MATERIALS

Magazines, newspaper pictures. Flip chart and pens.

PROCEDURE

The group leader may need to check that the word 'relationship' means the same thing to everyone; this may be the starting point of the session.

Using the picture material, people think of as many kinds of relationships as they can, for example:

▶ mother and baby

▶ husband and wife

▶ doctor and patient

The group leader's knowledge of people's environment can be used to draw out relevant relationships such as:

▶ home leader and residents

▶ teacher and student

▶ shop assistant and customer

A list is drawn up of all these relationships and put on the wall.

FORMAL OR INFORMAL

MATERIALS

Picture material and the lists of relationships generated in *What is a Relationship? (p.89)*. Flip chart and pens.

PROCEDURE

It may be appropriate to check that the words formal and informal have the same meaning to everyone in the group. Where applicable the titles could be changed.

The relationship types from the previous exercise are all written out on separate cards. The group leader assists people in deciding which category each relationship goes into. For example:

Formal	*Informal*
doctor – patient	friend – friend
bus conductor – passenger	father – son

LOOK AT THEM!

MATERIALS

A varied selection of photographs or slides of pairs and groups of people in formal and informal settings. Flip chart and pens.

PROCEDURE

The group leader reminds people of the non-verbal means of communication (*see What is a feeling? p.69*):

a) facial expression

b) posture

c) gesture

d) appearance

(The heading of voice is omitted in this activity.)

As the group looks at each photograph they discuss the non-verbal information they can see to decide if the relationship is formal or informal.

For example, a photograph showing soldiers on a parade ground, might be described in the following way:

▶ facial expression – neutral

▶ posture — – stiff, closed

▶ gesture — – practised drills

▶ appearance — – uniforms

LISTEN TO THEM!

MATERIALS

Tape recordings of people in conversation, dramas, announcers, disc jockeys, news readers and so on.

PROCEDURE

The group leader plays the tape. Participants discuss what the relationship is, based on *What* is said and also *How* it is said.

It may be appropriate to introduce the group to features such as intonation, volume and phrasing.

MY RELATIONSHIPS

MATERIALS

Pens and paper.

PROCEDURE

Each person takes time to think of the important relationships with people that they have now, or have had in the past. They then make a list of these, eg.

parents,

sister,

best friend.

THE GOOD AND THE BAD

MATERIALS

Flip chart and pens.

PROCEDURE

First the group breaks up into smaller groups or pairs to discuss what makes any relationship *good* and what makes any relationship *bad*.

After a time, the group joins up and brainstorms all the things that can make a relationship go bad or make it good. These are written down on to two flip charts and pinned up for everyone to see.

MAPS

MATERIALS

Blank paper and pens.

PROCEDURE

Each person draws a large circle on their sheet of paper, they then put a cross in the middle and write their name below it.

Next they put the names of the people they know at a distance from the centre that represents the quality of the relationship (*see Figure 3.5*).

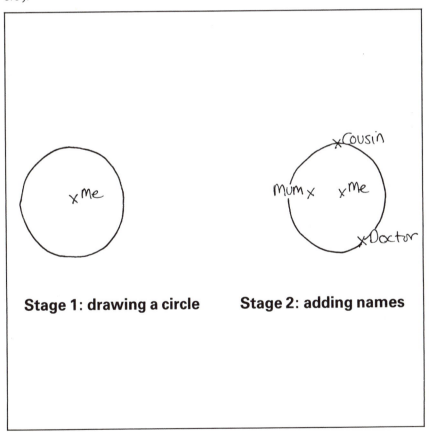

Stage 1: drawing a circle   **Stage 2: adding names**

Figure 3.5   *What are my relationships?*

MY EXPERIENCE

MATERIALS

None.

PROCEDURE

Each person takes a turn at talking to the rest of the group about one relationship they had which did not work out well and one relationship they made which was a success.

STARTERS

MATERIALS

A few props like glasses, jewellery, hats, cups and plates, tables and chairs. A prepared list of conversation starters relevant to the group's experience.

PROCEDURE

The group divides into pairs. Each pair is given a conversation starter, they are instructed to use this and then carry on the conversation. Some examples are given below:

1 *Setting* Post Office
  People Staff behind counter and customer.
  Starter (customer) "Hello, can you help me? I need . . ."

2 *Setting* Travel Agents
  People Staff behind counter and customer.
  Starter (staff) "Are you looking for a holiday?"

3 *Setting* Pub
  People Two customers standing at the bar.
  Starter (one customer to other) "I know you, it's John isn't it?"

4 *Setting* Bus queue
  People One person standing in queue, another person walks up.
  Starter "Excuse me, have you seen a brown dog, he's run off . . ."

5 *Setting* Swimming pool entrance – CLOSED
  People Two people carrying sports bags.
  Starter "Oh no! It's closed. I don't believe it . . ."

6 *Setting* Dentist's waiting room
  People Two patients waiting.
  Starter "I'm terrified, I hate having to come here . . ."

7 *Setting* Waiting area at a bank
  People Bank staff and a customer.
  Starter (bank staff) "Come in, Mr Grey. Sit down please. Now, about this bank loan . . ."

8 *Setting* High Street
  People Two friends meet.
  Starter (one friend) "Hello, I haven't seen you for ages, how are you?"

OVER THE TOP

MATERIALS

Video camera, flip chart and pens.

PROCEDURE

The purpose of this activity is to show people what *not* to do in conversations by going 'over the top' with some of the following conversation pitfalls (as discussed earlier in the section).

a) Looking bored;

b) Poor eye contact;

c) Blank face;

d) Inappropriate use of touch.

People are divided up into pairs to work out a short scene where one of the pair goes 'over the top'. The scenes are videoed and shown to the group.

After each scene, participants note down on flip charts as many of the pitfalls as they can, as well as noting the effects these have had on the other speaker.

NOW SAY IT AGAIN

MATERIALS

Video camera.

PROCEDURE

In this activity people enact the scenes from *Over the Top (p.98)*, correcting the mistakes.

As a variation to using the video, participants could be grouped in threes with one acting as an observer to give feedback to the others.

ALL TOGETHER

MATERIALS

An assortment of clothing props, furniture, cups, plates and so on. Flip chart and pens, video camera.

PROCEDURE

The whole group gets together to plan a short scene where everybody is involved.

People may invent their own story or they may prefer to adapt a well-known story, news item or television series.

NEW BEGINNINGS

MATERIALS

None.

PROCEDURE

Each person thinks of any changes that they wish to make in their relationships. This may mean a change in the way they behave when they meet someone again. It could mean reviving an old relationship that has broken down.

MATERIALS

An assortment of props.

PROCEDURE

Each person is encouraged to identify one communication situation which has been difficult for them. This could be from the past, the present or the future. Examples:

1   From the past. "There was a teacher at school who always picked on me."

2   From the present. "My sister is really worried about me living in the flat. She keeps fussing around."

3   From the future. "I have an interview for a place at college next month."

Once the situation has been identified, people act out what they wish they had said or plan to say in the future. The group leader should take the role of the other person.

NOTICE

MATERIALS

None.

PROCEDURE

At the end of a group meeting each person agrees to observe one social encounter before the next meeting and be ready to tell everyone about it.

Things to look out for are:

1 What the people talked about;
2 How they spoke to each other;
3 Use of body language.

LINK UP

MATERIALS

Relevant leaflets, brochures, posters.

PROCEDURE

As a result of the activities in this section, people may want to think of ways of increasing opportunities to meet and talk to other people.

Information on local groups, meetings and clubs may be presented to the group:

▶ lists of local clubs and groups people could join;

▶ sports clubs;

▶ linking up with local volunteers to provide an escort/befriending service for people to go to theatres, cinemas, pubs, bingo, shopping, day trips and so on.

COMPLEX SOCIAL COMMUNICATION

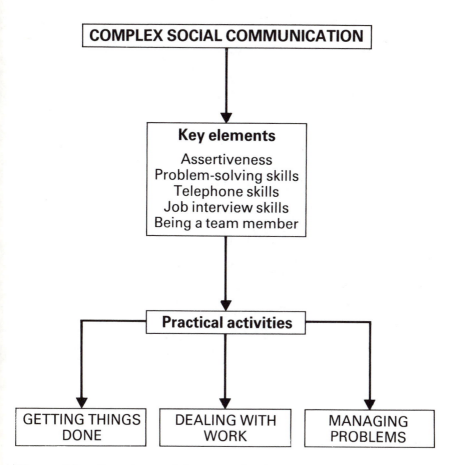

Figure 4.1 *Complex social communication*

WHAT ARE COMPLEX SOCIAL COMMUNICATION SKILLS?

With sufficient time and practice, group members may progress on to more complex social communication skills, pertinent to a range of everyday community settings.

The challenge here for group leaders is to provide a programme that enables group members to confront novel social situations and to help individuals develop their own repertoire of skills. There is always a choice of how one can respond in a given situation.

Also, at this level of social communication it is useful to explore face-saving devices or plausible social 'escape routes'. Most of us can recall without too much trouble our most recent social gaffe or embarrassing moment. Though we tend to dwell on the situation itself, perhaps we ought to examine more closely how we managed to retrieve our self-esteem without any dire consequences.

These face-saving devices may be such off-the-cuff techniques as being able to give a plausible excuse, cracking a topical joke or being adept at changing the subject. The socially competent individual is usually highly skilled at coping with this type of situation with aplomb.

Real mastery of complex communication skills is the 'icing on the cake' of everyday social interaction. Most of us are still learning and refining our social communication skills in an ever increasing range of new and demanding social situations. It is important for group members to not only master the skills and techniques, but to be initiated to the short cuts and 'hot tips' that may not be such a part of their knowledge or experience.

ASSERTIVENESS

CHARACTERISTICS

1 Assertiveness is . . .

   a) Being honest with yourself and acknowledging what you really feel.

   b) Being honest with others, without getting sidetracked.

   c) Being able to give and receive praise and criticism.

   d) Being respectful of other people's feelings.

2 Assertiveness is . . .

   a) 'How to say it straight without hurting others' (**Porritt**, 1985).

   b) 'The capacity to assert yourself is an important part of defining yourself in relationships' (**Nelson-Jones**, 1986).

TOO MUCH

The 'over-assertive' person is often perceived as being aggressive or 'pushy'; they may try to get what they want regardless of the consequences.

Over-assertiveness comes across as being insistent and dogmatic without considering a possible change of direction or alternative options. There may also be a seeming inability to work out a compromise if necessary.

TOO LITTLE

The 'under-assertive' individual may have a tendency to:

a) Blame others and not own up to their part in the relationship or situation.

b) Comply with others' wishes to avoid conflict, showing a fear of losing friends and often a denial of true feelings.

c) Feel guilty after saying 'no' – giving in to someone else's demands.

TARGET

1 To back up your verbal message with confident body language by:

    a) Maintaining eye contact;

    b) Having an open, relaxed posture;

    c) Reinforcing gestures and facial expression.

2 To say 'yes' when you mean 'yes', speaking clearly and directly.

3 To say 'no' when you mean 'no' and sticking to it.

4 To use appropriate assertive behaviour and thereby avoid the build-up of resentment and misunderstandings (eg. being taken for granted).

PROBLEM SOLVING

CHARACTERISTICS

Problem solving skills build on:

a) Past experience: learning from a previous similar situation;

b) Current experiences: present aptitudes and abilities;

c) Insight: the ability to anticipate the likely consequences of any solutions.

TOO MUCH

A rigid approach to problem solving may show itself in the following ways:

a) Sticking to a previous method of solving a problem without having evaluated its effectiveness.

b) Being insensitive to other people's needs: turning the solution into a series of 'musts'.

c) The inability to adjust and compromise: it is impossible to find a one hundred per cent perfect solution.

TOO LITTLE

The individual who is frightened of taking risks and 'rocking the boat' may accept their problems rather than try out possible new solutions. They may ignore or minimize a problem, hoping it will go away: instead the problem may get worse!

The difficulties of problem solving are increased if someone is not well-informed; it is important to collect all available information before deciding on the most appropriate course of action.

TARGET

1   The ability to clearly define what the problem is and a desire to solve it effectively.

2   The pooling of resources and skills can be fruitful – two heads are better than one and friends may provide valuable advice and support.

3   Being sensitive and aware of others' feelings as there can be a right time and place to confront a problem.

4   Being able to think creatively of possible solutions and select the most appropriate: one which is practical, guarantees success and is easy to implement.

TELEPHONE SKILLS

CHARACTERISTICS

1 An effective telephone manner is useful for:
  a) Keeping in touch with friends and relatives;
  b) Arranging visits and maintaining leisure interests;
  c) Making appointments (eg. dentist, doctor);
  d) Work situations (giving and receiving messages).
2 It is important to speak clearly and precisely, as no body language can be seen to back up and complement the verbal message.

TOO MUCH

Some behaviours to avoid when using the telephone are:

a) Speaking too quickly or too loudly, making the message difficult to follow.

b) Getting impatient if you do not get through to the right department or person straight away.

c) Slamming down the telephone and finishing the call abruptly – end on a pleasant, informal note if possible.

TOO LITTLE

It is important not to sound bored or uninterested; aim to have 'a smile in your voice' and show that you are actively listening. Use of the occasional comment ("Really? How interesting! And then. . .?") shows that you are still there and haven't gone off to make a cup of tea!

Being unprepared and not having available any relevant information (eg. important dates, names of people or a meeting place) conveys a poor impression.

TARGET

1 Prepare what to say in advance by having a list of key points.

2 Decide on the opening sentence to avoid getting flustered.

3 Say who you are and why you are calling.

4 Remember to use people's names where possible to add a more personal touch.

5 Record any useful information immediately after the phone call such as a date or time, place name, 'phone number.

JOB INTERVIEWS

CHECKLIST

1 Filling in application forms: requirements

a) Name, address
b) Position applied for
c) Education and training
d) Health
e) Details of present job and reasons for leaving
f) Previous jobs
g) Names and addresses of referees

2 Preparation

a) Why are you interested in this job?
b) Do you have any relevant experience?
c) What skills do you have from previous jobs?
d) Plan your route and method of transport.
e) Plan what you are going to wear – first impressions do count!

3 The interview

a) Initial social exchanges: 'ice breakers', getting-to-know-you phase. The overall manner is more important than actual content.
b) Job negotiation: deciding if you fit the job; being able to 'sell' yourself and being honest about strengths and limitations.

4 The right interview impression

a) Be enthusiastic and positive;
b) Express yourself clearly;
c) Be well informed about the job and the work place;
d) Be presentable;
e) Be confident: maintain eye contact, say more than 'yes' or 'no';
f) Be able to get on with other people.

BEING A TEAM MEMBER

CHECKLIST

Working in a team requires a balance of self-interest (own aspirations and needs) and team interest (working towards a common goal).

1 Functions of teams

a) Task oriented
  ▶ achieving set goals
  ▶ maintaining standards
  ▶ allocating different tasks to different team members;
b) Team maintenance
  ▶ clear channels of communication
  ▶ being kept informed and up-to-date
  ▶ regular contact and meetings;
c) Individual needs
  ▶ opportunities for privacy
  ▶ responding to individual differences
  ▶ acknowledging aptitudes and abilities.

2 Building on team spirit

a) A cohesive group (five to seven members) of similar age, sex and background;
b) Complementary personalities;
c) Opportunities to meet regularly;
d) Can communicate openly and clearly;
e) Can be flexible;
f) Encouragement of team loyalty and commitment;
g) Receive positive feedback from each other and from employers;
h) Feel a sense of pride in the contribution of the team.

3 Barriers to effective team work

a) Inappropriate or ineffective leadership;
b) Lack of group commitment;
c) Uncertainty about common goal, either its purpose or how to achieve it;
d) Ineffective work methods and organization;
e) Stifling of any creative or original ideas;
f) An unconstructive work atmosphere (tension, silences, disagreements, criticism).

PRACTICAL ACTIVITIES

GETTING THINGS DONE

Aims
1 To encourage purposeful social communication in order to achieve some activity necessary for independent daily living.
2 To increase awareness of a positive approach to social communication.

List of Practical Activities

WHAT AM I DOING?

MATERIALS

Props.

PROCEDURE

The group observes the leader miming daily living activities. Examples:

▶ going to the shops
▶ visiting the library
▶ making tea
▶ washing dishes
▶ doing the laundry
▶ cleaning
▶ cooking dinner

Members have to guess the activity and try miming it themselves. A more advanced way might be to introduce errors for people to notice.

COMMERCIAL BREAK

MATERIALS

None.

PROCEDURE

Imagine being on a shelf in a shop. Think of why someone should buy you.

▶ Who are you?

▶ What are you worth?

▶ What are you good at?

▶ What skills are you willing to learn?

I SEE, I THINK

MATERIALS

Pictures, video material, drawings, photos, people in uniforms.

PROCEDURE

Using clothing, video and pictorial material, ask the group to identify what they see. Members may comment on occupation, style, age, personality, appropriateness and so on.

Examples of what people might say are:

"I see a white coat."

"This person's very modern."

"I think they're going out to do the garden."

USING THE TELEPHONE

MATERIALS

Catalogues, pamphlets.

PROCEDURE

Visits may be arranged to local showrooms and exchanges to look at various kinds of telephones and their operation. Consideration might be needed in deciding on the best type of telephone to suit individuals such as push button, memory, ansaphones and amplification.

ANSWER ME!

MATERIALS

Stopwatch, telephones.

PROCEDURE

Vary the length of time the telephone rings, gradually increasing it using the stopwatch as a guide.

Ask members:

a) How does it feel to have to wait for a reply?

b) How does it feel not to immediately answer the telephone?

c) What do you think the other person is thinking?

d) Why might someone take a long time to answer?

I WANT, I WISH

MATERIALS

Pictures (optional).

PROCEDURE

Everyone sits in a circle. One person turns to the next and says "I want to . . .". The person listening says "What do you need?" and the person replies. The listener then turns to the person the other side of him or her and says, "I want to . . ." and so on.

This activity may also be carried out by assigning an A, B or C label to people. All A people make a statement starting, "I need . . .". All B people make a statement starting "I want . . ." and all C people make a statement starting "I wish . . .".

The aim is to establish whether or not there are any activities that members could work towards trying out.

IT'S NOT WHAT YOU SAY . . .

MATERIALS

Photos or pictures showing feelings and emotions.

PROCEDURE

Each member brainstorms a 'feeling' word which they enact non-verbally. The feeling can be passed on to the next person and so on for each person to mirror.

The leader suggests or elicits expressions for particular activities. Examples are:

▶ Can you help me?
▶ What's the time?
▶ Where is the bus stop?

NOSY NEIGHBOURS

MATERIALS

Bean bag.

PROCEDURE

One member throws a bean bag to another member whilst calling out the person's name. The recipient tries to describe what they know about the thrower's daily activities and routines.

GREETINGS AND COMPLIMENTS

MATERIALS

Pictures, symbols, phrases.

PROCEDURE

In a group people take turns to give a greeting or compliment to each other. Comments may be about a coming birthday, personality, clothing, something that has been done which is appreciated and so on. These may be spontaneous or picture clues, symbols or phrases may be put down on paper for members to 'fit' to a person in the group. Examples:

▶ Happy birthday

▶ I like your dress

▶ I hope you feel better soon

▶ Thank you for helping me with . . .

The recipient of the comment practices accepting it. If this is difficult then this is discussed.

WHAT NEXT?

MATERIALS

Pictures or objects which suggest an activity, such as a shoe, radiator, milk bottle or telephone.

PROCEDURE

An object or picture is presented to the group, eg. a shoe. The leader may say, "I need my shoe repaired, so I . . .". Members of the group add to the sentence what they think should happen next.

The group may eventually generate ideas of potential problems when picking an object from a tray, bag, or box.

GROUP GRIEVANCES

MATERIALS

A video camera, construction materials to build a model of a house.

PROCEDURE

Pieces of paper are given out with a picture, symbol or written description showing a particular behaviour. Examples:

▶ compulsive talking

▶ talking loudly

▶ mumbling

▶ criticizing

▶ withdrawing

▶ sulking

The group tries out the behaviours in a house-building activity which is videoed. This is then played back for discussion of individual behaviours and their effects.

The activity may be tried again using members' preferred behaviours. Members may suggest different behaviours to others for trying out.

LIFE STYLES

MATERIALS

Appointment cards, diaries and props.

PROCEDURE

In turn members describe typical daily routines to the group and say what is 'good' about their day and what could be improved. Others are invited to ask questions and suggest ways of overcoming difficulties.

Examples of activities are: getting up late or forgetting a travel pass and so on.

ACTION PLAN

MATERIALS

Charts, diaries, notepads.

PROCEDURE

Individuals work out an achievement that really matters to them and they talk it through with a partner. Questions the partner might ask are:

"How will you know you've got there?"

"What might you do to spoil things for yourself?"

"What support do you need?"

"How will you get it?"

DEALING WITH WORK

Aims

1   To encourage effective social communication appropriate for the work place.
2   To explore the requirements of working collaboratively with other people.

List of practical activities

Looking and Listening to Others
Looking and Listening to Ourselves
Try it Out

WHO'S WHO?

MATERIALS

Video, photos.

PROCEDURE

Video material and role-plays are shown to the group for them to identify the kind of work relationship people have. Some may be satisfactory, others unsatisfactory, some formal, others informal. Examples:

▶ shop assistant and customer

▶ police officer and member of the public

▶ boss and worker

▶ worker and union representative

WHICH JOB?

MATERIALS

Props, pictures, photos.

PROCEDURE

One person mimes an action associated with a particular job. Another person describes the activity. Further miming might give more clues to the answer, or multiple-choice picture representations could be used.

Examples:

▶ traffic warden

▶ typist

▶ shop assistant

TEAMWORK

MATERIALS

Video.

PROCEDURE

Members observe a group of people, live or on video, who are building a house from boxes, paper, tubing, and so on.

Afterwards members try to work out who was:

a) the leader
b) the deputy leader
c) the worker
d) the ideas person
e) the saboteur

The behaviours which helped members recognize these roles are identified.

FORMING, STORMING

MATERIALS

Video.

PROCEDURE

A video of a team activity is shown to the group. Afterwards, members are asked to describe what happened. Encouragement can be given by asking questions such as:

How successful was the team in achieving the task?

What were they like in the beginning? Friendly? Hostile? Anxious? Quiet? Withdrawn?

How did they become later on?

When did they appear to start working?

What happened then?

SPECIAL NEEDS

MATERIALS

Bean bags.

PROCEDURE

Members throw bean bags to each other; whoever catches it tells the group what needs they have at work. The activity can be changed by getting the person catching to describe the needs they think the person throwing the bag has.

SPACES

MATERIALS

Various chairs and tables.

PROCEDURE

Group members divide into pairs. One pair enacts an interview situation, taking on the roles of employee and employer. The employee practices making particular requests to the employer, using different body language and seating positions. Here are some different seating arrangements that may be used:

a) Employer standing, employee sitting;

b) Employer sitting on a higher chair than employee;

c) Sitting directly opposite each other or sitting at right angles;

d) Sitting on easy chairs;

e) Sitting across a large table on high-backed chairs.

Each role-play is discussed and different responses noted.

COLOUR GAME

MATERIALS

A video camera, paper.

PROCEDURE

The group divides into two teams, one role-plays, the other observes. The role-playing team has to decide on a colour in five minutes. Only one colour will do. Each person is told or given a piece of paper with a word, symbol, or picture of a particular behaviour which they must enact whilst role-playing the choice of colour. Examples of behaviours are:

a) You do not mind what colour is chosen as long as you can get away early.

b) You disagree with every suggestion made.

c) You agree with everyone else's suggestion.

d) You try to take charge.

e) You withdraw from the group.

After five minutes a colour must be decided upon. The observing team tries to work out who was doing what and the 'actors' confess. Video feedback may help the discussion.

MATERIALS

None.

PROCEDURE

In a group one person says to the person opposite or next to them "Hello, how are you?" When a response is elicited that person turns to the person opposite or next to them and gives the same greeting.

After a while, members try out other types of greetings. In pairs, Person A says "Hello, how are you?" and Person B says "Good news or bad news first?" After exchanges are made, the pair swap round. Members gradually move round the circle. In later activities the conversation might be developed.

BLOW YOUR OWN TRUMPET

MATERIALS

None.

PROCEDURE

Decide on a possible job or activity, then members take turns to say why they might be good at doing it. For example:

"I'd be good at washing cars because . . ."

"I'd be good at being a nurse because . . ."

The idea is to encourage members to recognize abilities they have and whether they are likely to use them in a specified occupation or not.

The activity can be extended to "I wouldn't be good at it because . . .". Skills that might need developing can be discussed and worked on in future activities.

ON SET

MATERIALS

Video, building materials such as glue, string, scissors, sellotape, paper and crayons.

PROCEDURE

This activity is similar to *Teamwork* (*see p. 139*). The group carries out a house-building activity which is either observed live or on video.

The members are asked to comment on what they thought of themselves and whether or not they felt happy with getting the task done. Participants are asked if they would like to change any behaviours and have the opportunity to try the activity again. Members then comment on each other; observers provide feedback and suggestions.

SAFARI

MATERIALS

Tables, chairs, pen and paper (optional).

PROCEDURE

Half the group acts as interviewees and the other half as interviewers. The task of the interviewers is to select the most suitable candidate for a safari holiday to travel with six other people.

The interviewers have separate tables and chairs. The interviewees go round each interviewer and spend five minutes with them being interviewed on why they think they are the best person for the job.

The interviewers may be given a set of questions to ask which the interviewees can prepare for. Examples of topics are:

▶ cooking skills
▶ ability to get on with people
▶ health

When everyone has had a turn, the most suitable person's name is given to the leader outside the room or written on a piece of paper and the winner is announced. The group can then discuss what helped the person win.

MANAGING PROBLEMS

Aims
1 To use social communication skills to clarify and resolve everyday problems.
2 To identify useful facilities and resources within the community.

List of practical activities

CAN I HELP YOU?

MATERIALS

Pictures, photos, videos.

PROCEDURE

Visual material of people and occupational groups, which the members are likely to come into contact with, is handed out to the group. Key expressions are called out for members to match their picture to. Examples:

"Can I help you?"

"May I see your bag?"

"Ticket please"

"This way"

"We close in ten minutes"

"Next please."

"Enquiries. What name please?"

"Operator service. Can I help?"

The activity may change to members calling out an expression for others to guess the person or occupation.

Video material may be used to observe interactions between members of the public, television characters and those carrying out a job.

SPOT THE RISK

MATERIALS

Fire extinguisher, fire blanket, matches, chip pan, cigarette, various alarms, wastepaper basket, bag, purse, banana skin, ashtray.

PROCEDURE

This activity should be carried out with local emergency service officers (fire, ambulance, police).

Send everyone out of the room, having explained that when they return they have to spot the potential risk. Examples:

▶ A cigarette left burning in an ashtray or wastebin.

▶ A purse left on a table near an open window.

▶ A handbag casually left open.

▶ A chip pan on the stove with oil nearby.

▶ A banana skin on the floor.

▶ An adaptor with lots of plugs attached.

▶ A long electric flex stretched from a table lamp to the socket.

▶ Tablets and medicines in a box on the floor.

▶ Bleach and other cleaning fluids in an open cupboard at floor level.

EMERGENCY SERVICES

MATERIALS

Health and safety material, slides.

PROCEDURE

Invite ambulance, fire and police officers to give talks on health and safety, relating this to emergency services and dialling 999.

Ensure that tapes can be stopped and 'gone over' to reinforce messages. Allow time for questions. Try to ask questions along the way to ensure that the material has been understood.

Allow the opportunity for those who may have witnessed a fire, theft or accident to say so and talk about what happened.

I HAVE A PROBLEM

MATERIALS

Photos and pictures.

PROCEDURE

Ask the group what problems different people might have with their work and discuss what might help them to overcome their problems. Examples:

▶ police officer
▶ nurse
▶ secretary
▶ gardener

EMERGENCIES

MATERIALS

Telephones, card, pens, picture frames, a flip chart, photographs and pictures. Health and safety audio-visual and pamphlet material.

PROCEDURE

This activity could be combined with or follow on from a talk by an emergency officer.

The word 'emergency' is written on a flip chart. Members are asked to say what they think the word means and to give examples. 'Fire', 'Police' and 'Ambulance' are then presented on the flip chart and each one is discussed. For example:

Fire

What causes a fire?

How do you know there is a fire?

How do you raise the alarm?

What do you do then?

The activity should relate to individuals, groups and their particular environments and environments encountered.

Telephoning 999

What are the 999 services for?

When do you use it?

Who answers the phone?

What do they say?

What do you say?

Questions may be combined or replaced by giving 'clues'. For example:

"If someone drops a cigarette and it carries on burning what might happen?"

LATERAL THINKING

MATERIALS

Pictures or photos of different problem situations (eg. a man standing beside a broken door and looking upset).

PROCEDURE

Present examples of situations to the group and ask them how the situation might have arisen (in the above example, the door might have been the result of a couple having an argument and a partner slamming the door).

BE CAREFUL

MATERIALS

Photos, videos and props.

PROCEDURE

A situation is observed. It can be either role-played, watched on video or seen in photos. The group is asked to think of things that could go wrong and then to discuss what might help the situation to go well.

PROBLEM GENERATION

MATERIALS

A flip chart, marker pens, pictures and photos.

PROCEDURE

If pictorial material is used, it should be distributed to the group. Members call out a possible problem from what they see.

Suggested problems are written up and may be used for discussion in later activities such as *First Aid (p.159)*, *Agony Aunt (p.161)* or *Who Can Help? (p.163)*.

FIRST AID

MATERIALS

First-aid kit and its contents.

PROCEDURE

Talk about different minor injuries and discuss how a first-aid kit might be used. General advice on how to deal with headaches, backache, toothache and so on might be tackled.

RED ALERT!

MATERIALS

Telephones, card, felt pens, glue, sellotape, cellophane, clip-frames and scissors.

PROCEDURE

Each person makes their own emergency card to carry around with them and to display in appropriate places. Here is an example of an emergency card:

EMERGENCY	
FIRE	999
AMBULANCE	999
POLICE	999
In case of emergency/accident please contact	
1. Lift telephone receiver.	
2. Dial or press 999.	

AGONY AUNT

MATERIALS

Letters from problem pages, or invented ones, about practical or emotional problems.

PROCEDURE

A problem is read out to the group for them to discuss the advice that they would offer.

TOWER OF STRENGTH

MATERIALS

None.

PROCEDURE

Discuss ways in which members get help with their problems and consider how support can be gained. In pairs, members practice asking for help with a problem.

WHO CAN HELP?

MATERIALS

Photos, pictures, symbols, pens, diaries and cards.

PROCEDURE

Members think of a real or imaginary problem and discuss who can help outside the group. Those people can be invited to the group to discuss the problems put to them.

MATERIALS

Notebooks and pens. A resource file of useful addresses.

PROCEDURE

Members discuss how to follow up information relevant to their needs. Information may relate to work (paid or unpaid), housing rights, health or other issues. Useful resources:

► Public library
► Citizens Advice Bureau (CAB)
► Law centre or legal advice centre
► Local councillor or Member of Parliament (MP)
► Consumers' Association
► Voluntary agencies

Example: work-related rights
Whom would you ask about the following situations?
How would you ask about the following situations?

► annual leave
► overtime
► pay-slips
► wage increases
► holidays
► health and safety regulations
► smoking policies
► application forms
► sick leave

► union membership
► being late/absent
► compassionate leave
► hospital/dental appointments
► incidents/accidents procedure
► fire regulations
► benefits

Further Information

Patients' Rights: a guide to the rights and responsibilities of patients and doctors in the National Health Service (a National Consumer Council publication).

TWO HEADS ARE BETTER THAN ONE

MATERIALS

Paper and pens.

PROCEDURE

Two people in the group plan an activity or outing and say aloud how they plan to do it. They then ask another member of the group to add further information on how to pursue the activity.

BILLBOARD

MATERIALS

Magazine pictures, large sheets of paper or card, felt pens, paints, crayons, pencils, glue, sellotape, scissors and drawing pins.

PROCEDURE

Each person makes a poster using magazine pictures, drawings or any materials at hand to advertise their skills for their job placement.

REFERENCES

Adler RB & Rodman G, *Understanding Human Communication* (3rd edn), Holt, Reinhart & Winston, London, 1988.

Argyle M, 'Some New Developments in Social Skills Training,' Mayor BM & Pugh AK (eds), *Language, Communication and Education*, Croom Helm, London, 1987.

Berne E, *Transactional Analysis in Psychotherapy*, Souvenir Press, London, 1975.

Hargie O, Saunders C & Dickson D, *Social Skills in Interpersonal Communication*, Croom Helm, London, 1981.

Longabough R *et al*, 'The Interactional World of the Chronic Schizophrenic Patient,' Argyle M, *Social Interaction*, Tavistock Publications, London, 1969.

Maslow AH, *Motivation and Personality* (3rd edn), Harper & Row, New York, 1987.

Nelson-Jones R, *Human Relationship Skills*, Cassell, London, 1986.

Porritt L, *Communication Choices for Nurses*, Churchill Livingstone, Edinburgh, 1985.

Schutz W, 'The Interpersonal World,' Adler RB & Rodman G (eds), *Understanding Human Communication* (3rd edn), Holt, Reinhart & Winston, London, 1988.

Tuckman BW, 'Developmental Sequences in Small Groups', Handy CB, *Understanding Organisations* (2nd edn), Penguin Books, Middlesex, 1981.

Zimbardo PG, 'Shyness,' Nelson-Jones R, *Human Relationship Skills*, Cassell, London, 1986.

BIBLIOGRAPHY

Annett J et al , Ellis R & Whittington D (eds), *A Guide to Social Skills Training*, Croom Helm, London, 1981.

Argyle M, *The Psychology of Interpersonal Behaviour* (4th edn), Penguin Books, Middlesex, 1983.

Breakwell GM, Foot H & Gilmour R, *Social Psychology: A Practical Manual*, Macmillan, London, 1982.

Curran JP & Monti PM (eds), *Social Skills Training*, Guildford Press, New York, 1982.

Hargie O (ed), *A Handbook of Communication Skills*, Croom Helm, London, 1986.

Harris TA, *I'm OK — You're OK*, Pan, London, 1973.

Hjelle LA & Ziegler DJ, *Personality Theories* (2nd edn), McGraw-Hill, Maidenhead, 1988.

Kagan C, Evans J & Kay B, *A Manual of Interpersonal skills for Nurses: an Experiential Approach*, Harper & Row, London, 1986.

Pope B, *Social Skills Training for Psychiatric Nurses*, Harper & Row, London, 1986.

Sharpe R, *Assert Yourself* (2nd edn), Kogan Page, London, 1989.

Warr P (ed), *Psychology at Work* (3rd edn), Penguin Books, Middlesex, 1987.

Wilkinson J & Canter S, *Social Skills Training Manual*, John Wiley & Sons, Chichester, 1982.

INDEX TO ACTIVITIES